novum pro

Brigitta Rhyner

The Fine Art of Old Age Living Well and Dying Well

A Guide for relatives and auxiliary staff

novum pro

ISBN 978-3-99131-496-7
Cover photo:
Anna Om | Dreamstime.com
Cover design, layout & typesetting:
novum publishing
Author's photo: Foto Winiger GmbH

www.novumpublishing.com

Climate neutral
Print product
ClimatePartner.com/16547-2201-1002

An insight into the everyday life of care home residents in their autumn days

Being a companion for the painful process of letting go

Respectful interaction at the end of life

Contents

Dedication

A homage to the many dear people that I have been able to accompany on their last journey over the years.

I would like to thank the countless people who have allowed me to accompany them on their last journey into another dimension and with some even up to their physical death.

Introduction

Before I trained as a dying companion, I had, over a period of ten years, accompanied four loved family members and a friend as they approached their death.

When I think back to these journeys, I often wish that I knew back then what I now know about terminal and palliative care.
I would have dealt more professionally with the approaching signs of death. Instead, back then, I felt quite helpless and at a loss.

These private dying experiences made me want to delve deeper into this subject. They showed me, that I was missing important practical information for a better grasp and understanding.

These experiences laid the foundation for starting a three-year training course to become a death and grief counsellor.

During my training I came across an advertisement:
"Voluntary companion to the dying wanted"
So began my work as a death and grief counsellor to the dying in a nursing home.

In the last ten years, through this work I have got to know and appreciate many different, wonderful, loving, grateful and sometimes challenging elderly people.

I was allowed to accompany some of them not only during their everyday lives in a care home, but also in their last days, up to their death.

Some time ago I received an unexpected request from a publisher as to whether I would like to write a book about my experiences as a dying companion and grief counsellor. After initially being astonished, I was fascinated by this idea.

I decided to write a guide in which I describe my work as a death and grief counsellor in a nursing home as well as report on everyday life in the care home with all its facets and address a taboo topic, the dying process.

I thought hard about which topics would interest or be of help to a wider audience.

The book focuses on the situation of people who, voluntarily or forced by external circumstances, enter a care institution, and spend the rest of their days there until they die.

In this guide, I also pay close attention to the relatives, as the terminal care of a loved one is often an unknown and frightening time for them.

I am aware, that for a large part of the population the subject of illness, entering a care home and dying is a taboo subject, but dying affects us all.

With this guide I would like to give you an insight into the practical side of the dying process and show you how you can calmly accompany and support your loved ones in this difficult and emotional phase for you both.

Whether they like it or not, many people will need to consider whether their loved ones must go into a nursing home.

It is too tempting to avoid considering the realities of life in a nursing home and how illnesses progress, the dying process and palliative care.

However, it is important to deal with these realities early because you never know when and what will happen to you in life, and death is part of life.

Like many people, I was forced to deal with this topic when my mother became seriously ill.

Part 1
Entering a care home

1.1. Challenge or relief?

Unfortunately, it is not uncommon for an elderly person to be admitted to a care facility after a medical emergency, without ever being able to enter their own home again and return to their old way of life.

This is a challenging situation and does not make it easy for those affected, to get used to the idea, that the nursing home will now be their home and their future life.

Most people are in denial about the possibility of a stay in a nursing home. They tell themselves that it will never be necessary, which is not always the case.

According to the BFS (the Swiss Federal Statistical Office), only around 15% of people over 80 live in a nursing home. The others are still independent or take advantage of other options. Nevertheless, you can never know in advance whether a care home may be necessary in your circumstances and so it is wise to consider care home options ahead of time, rather than be rushed in an emergency. This allows the home to be considered calmly and carefully.

Challenge

Entering a nursing home is a big step and a huge challenge, not only for those affected, but also for their relatives.

Life, which up to now has taken place in one's own home with a lot of freedom and independence, is now reduced to a room, that may have to be shared depending on the financial situation. What does this mean in concrete terms? I will go into this in more details in Sections 1.5 and 1.6.

Relief

For some people, however, entering a care institution is a great relief, especially when it has been a struggle to meet day to day needs at home.
Housework, cooking, shopping, organising etc are no longer necessary. Instead, depending on their state of health, a care home resident can gain new freedoms. Energy can be used for everyday activities such as walking, playing, reading, doing handicrafts, etc. Not to mention the healthcare and personal security and safety benefits. Support takes place around the clock! If necessary, a healthcare specialist can always be called in.

The relief is often noticeable in the relatives too, initially mixed with concern about how their loved ones will settle in.

To gently accustom the elderly to life in a care home, many homes offer respite stays. This can reduce acute fears or mitigate possible shock.

1.2. Involuntary care home admission

Where nursing home admission has been determined by others

As a result of accident or illness, many elderly people suddenly become unable to find their way mentally and physically. The situation may change very abruptly, possibly starting with a short or longer hospital stay, after which it may be clear that they are no longer able to return to living in their own home.

There will not have been the time to prepare mentally for entering a care home and a new life situation. The decision is thrust upon them with no time to adjust and perhaps without the patient being able to participate in the decision-making process.

There are various reasons that make it impossible for an elderly, sick person to be able to live at home again after a stay in hospital, eg; that they live alone or the health of their partner.

I will illustrate this to you using the example of my mother's illness:

My mother lived alone in an apartment. She kept feeling tired for many months. It got so bad that she couldn't get out of bed. I worked and did not live near her. Her neighbour called for the doctor and he referred her directly to the hospital. I visited my mother every day, while she was in hospital.

After a week my mother was told that she could go home several days later with home care support. I moved her room to the lower floor and was happy about this good news.

Two days later, the doctor told me that my mother's condition was worsening. She said that my mother would have to go to an old people's home. That same day I looked for a place and confirmed my mother's admission there.

The next day, the doctor explained to me that my mother's deteriorating condition now made it necessary to look for a place in a nursing home.

I was devastated. Functioning like a robot, I looked for a nursing home. At that point in time, I couldn't fully grasp what had just happened. It was unreal.

My mother would have to go to a care home without being able to participate in the decision-making process, she had no choice.

Residents told me that they had a lot of trouble not being able to slowly say goodbye to their own home and their old life. They found it difficult making decisions such as:

How do I give up my apartment?
Whom do I give things to?
Who will take care of my pet?
What do I want to take with me to the nursing home that is close to my heart and important to me?
What clothes do I take with me?

Up until now, the patient had full control over their life and decisions such as these.

If relatives or strangers make these decisions without fully involving the resident, they feel powerless, and it might trigger a great sadness and loss of dignity.

Sometimes the residents only notice much later that they are still missing a special piece of jewellery, a photo album, a certain book, or an item of clothing that they particularly like.

It is understandable if this causes frustration, resentment or sadness.

Careful, understanding interaction with a professional, relatives or nursing staff sometimes works wonders!

Alternatively, it may be that a care home admission is necessary because the patient's partner is overwhelmed by the care needs. Often it is not only the partner who is overwhelmed, but also the adult children who may not realise the level of care now required.

I would like to use two examples to show you that adult children cannot always judge or see exactly how their parents are coping, and whether they are still able to continue living independently at home without help.

As these two examples illustrate perception and reality may differ.

1. Example: An elderly woman lived alone in her apartment. She was diagnosed with Parkinson's years ago. She managed everything independently and her illness remained stable for a long time.
Her mental state slowly deteriorated – almost imperceptibly. It started with the fact that she misplaced things or could no longer find them. She covered this up for a long time and stayed vague in her statements. It took a long time before she could admit that her forgetfulness was increasing. The woman realized that she was forgetting important appointments and mixing up the dates. She no longer ate regularly, no longer cooked properly, forgot her medication, or took too much medication. Ultimately, this had health consequences.

Then home care support was organised, including food deliveries. Since the food was brought in long before mealtimes, the woman did not eat the food straight away, because she was not hungry. When she was hungry, she no longer knew that the food was ready in the frying pan and all she need do was warm it up. Nobody noticed this. As a result, the woman became weak and fell from balance problems.

Her son took good care of her. However, he could not live with her 24 hours a day. So, the real situation remained hidden for a long time, until one day the woman was admitted to the hospital because she fell again and was confused.

In the hospital it became clear that the woman could no longer live alone, and that after the hospital stay a place in a nursing home needed to be found and notice served on the apartment.

2. Example: An elderly couple lived at home. They had adult children. The father had dementia but could still do everything his wife asked him to do. The mother seemed clear in her head though she could hardly walk anymore and needed help. She had RLS (restless leg syndrome).

The children set it up so that the daughter visited the parents every Tuesday and one of her siblings on Sundays. The daughter then arranged for five dinners and the lunches to be brought by the meal service.

When the daughter visited her parents again the mother told her that she was hungry.
The daughter asked whether they had eaten the meal from the meal service at lunchtime.
She replied that they ate this a long time ago.

In the kitchen the daughter saw that the father had emptied the meals into the rubbish bin! The meal came so early that the father, because of his dementia, said he had to empty the pans and wash them up. Because of this, he kept throwing the food away without his wife noticing.

That night the daughter slept at her parents' house because she had the feeling that something was wrong. As a result she noticed what was going on in the night. The mother kept waking her husband because she had restless legs or had to go to the toilet.

It was only then, that the daughter realised that her parents were no longer able to live alone at home. The children therefore had to look for another solution.

With these examples I want to show that the situation is often misjudged, even when the children take good care of their parents.

1.3. Advanced care planning

In my opinion, it is imperative that every healthy person, no matter how old, carries out advanced care planning.

One never knows what will happen in life. An accident can happen, or one get seriously ill. People are not always able to communicate after an accident.

Discussions about life-sustaining measures or other treatments in an emergency should be conducted with relatives while in a healthy state and written down.

Questions can be asked such as:
If necessary, would I like to be connected to a heart-lung machine and only stay alive with a life support machine? If I fall into a coma, do I want the machines or do I not want them? Would I really want to have an operation at my age?
A Do not Resuscitate Form (DNR) can be discussed and filled out with the family doctor.

Having an agreed advanced care plan is a great relief, and an aid for relatives in an emergency. They have something documented, they know what their loved ones want and can, if necessary, hand this over to the emergency doctor, the paramedics, or the hospital. An advanced care plan needs to be kept readily available as copies may not be acceptable. Some people choose to have a copy stored on their medical records.

1.4. Sacrifice to the point of being overwhelmed

There are many different situations that can lead to excessive demands on a relative providing or enabling care at home.

An example: An elderly couple lived together at home in a harmonious relationship. One day one of the partners become bedridden and needed care. The healthy partner took over the organisation of the household, the cooking and taking care of the sick partner.

Being bedridden can trigger feelings of fear, sadness, anger and frustration over time.
Since the able partner is the closest confidante, these feelings are often taken out on them. The able partner may not feel as though they can share how they are affected with the person they are caring for, out of consideration for their illness, leaving them as a carer, with no emotional support. This can create a conflict-laden, emotionally unbearable situation that begins to burden the healthy partner, damaging the good relationship and affecting the able partner's health.

The changes in the delegation of duties can overwhelm a partner. The responsibility of running the household, going shopping, cooking and looking after the sick partner and fulfilling their wishes now rests solely on the healthy partner.

Often the patient prefers to be looked after and cared for in their own environment.
But what about the healthy partner?
For them it can become a great physical and psychological burden over time.

When the healthy partner reaches their physical limits, a new solution must be found that is fair to both parties.

It may not be perfect, but a care home may be an acceptable compromise.

It is better to have a partner who comes to visit the nursing home, who is rested and satisfied, rather than have both parties endure a conflict situation at home every day!

Generally, everyone feels staying at home is always the best place to be. However, for the sick person it is sometimes harder at home as they feel more dependent and powerless seeing their healthy partner do all the things they can no longer do.

An accident or illness of the mother or father can be a great challenge for relatives. They are faced with the situation of deciding what is the best solution for both parties:

To care for the sick person at home, for example together with a home-carer, or to consider a nursing home.

In my opinion, the relatives should think hard before they say yes to the great self-sacrificing task of caring for a relative at home. There is always the option later when death is imminent, that they may bring their loved one back home to die.

Relatives often feel guilty when thinking about a nursing home: "I can't just put my dear Mum or Dad into a nursing home!"

Even if the father or mother does not want to enter a nursing home, I advise everyone involved to think twice about it, because it is possible that a seriously ill person will still live for a long time and the care at home will, over time, overwhelm everyone's strength and possibly lead to burnout.

1.5. The adjustment phase to everyday life in a care home

I have observed that the initial adjustment phase is often quite challenging for the residents because of the high levels of uncertainty for them. Sometimes they are not very cooperative because they are in the transition phase, which is not easy for them.
Nursing staff, relatives and professionals must show great sensitivity.

A nursing home cannot provide completely personalised care. The residents must adapt to certain structured routines. This sometimes creates conflicts around mealtimes, shower times and bedtimes, because people may have had a different rhythm of life or daily routine at home. However, the care team will try to respond to the residents' requests as best they can, be it their getting up time or personal care, to accommodate the residents as much as possible.

It requires a willingness to compromise and adapt on the part of the residents and the nursing staff, which is easier for some and more difficult for others.

Before new residents can find their way around the home, there are often some hurdles to overcome. Which floor is my room on? Where is the dining room? Where is the exit to the garden? Where is the studio? Depending on their cognitive ability, this triggers stress or anxiety. The residents are often uncomfortable with disturbing the staff with questions.

The residents may be left to their own devices for a few hours, depending on their state of health, and are therefore confronted with important questions such as:
How do I make my everyday life satisfactory for me despite my health restrictions? Which activities and opportunities that the home offers, am I still interested in? What would I enjoy?

Most care institutions offer a variety of activities that can bring a welcome change for many residents.

How can residents, whose health no longer allows them to actively participate in what is happening, keep busy?

Depending on the health impairment, the staff may be able to use their imagination to think of creative ways to reduce the time residents spend on their own. For example, residents might be given small tasks such as laying the table.

I have observed that the happiest residents are those who find a way to accept their situation and try to make the best of it.

1.6. Loss of privacy

Entry into a care facility is a drastic change for anyone who has previously led an independent life. Suddenly they are confronted with new challenges of all kinds.

Since some residents are placed in a double room, due to room availability or financial reasons, they have to share their space with someone else, which means that their privacy is massively restricted.

Sleep quality and psychological well-being can be impaired if, for example, the roommate has a different sleep rhythm, or snores, or the nursing staff must check in several times during the night.

The loss of privacy is also fraught with stress and shame when residents need help to go to the toilet, are no longer able to shower or look after themselves and are dependent on the support of a carer.

The new resident must be given time to come to terms with this new and demanding dependent situation.

1.7. Challenges in everyday life in a care home

Cognitive/physical limitations

There are many reasons for entering a nursing home. For example, if a person is no longer able to carry out day to day activities, like cooking, required to take care of themselves. The reasons for this might be cognitive and / or physical limitations.
This might be as a result of a stroke or a brain haemorrhage or they may be bedridden for other health reasons. They may have fallen or are weak because of old age and they are no longer able to live alone. It may be that their hearing or eyesight has deteriorated drastically.

Many residents can therefore no longer take part in the activity programs due to health issues. They may get bored. The staff cannot take care of them one to one, although they would love to. However, the daily structure is tight and there is no time for longer individual care! This means that the residents are often left to their own devices for a long time and feel useless. They may feel no longer "needed" and dependent on the goodwill of other people.

It can also be challenging if a resident is physically impaired but still cognitively able. They may then find it difficult to make their everyday life "meaningful", whatever that means for the individual.

There is a danger in these scenarios that they may withdraw into themselves and lapse into lethargy or indifference.

Loneliness

There are also residents who are lonely because they either no longer have relatives to visit at regular intervals or because their relatives work or live in another city or even abroad – or the contact has been broken off.
It's twice as hard for these residents to maintain their positive attitude.

The residents are even more grateful when volunteers come to visit them and support them in various matters, such as visiting the doctor, shopping and walking, etc.

In my experience, every resident was so grateful to receive my full attention for a few hours, I listened to them when they wanted to talk and something bothered them or when they needed specific advice. They felt properly heard and taken seriously.

Sadness

Sometimes, personal circumstances have caused great sadness to a resident. This sadness may be as a result of moving to the care home, as a result of a deterioration in health or a loss of a partner. Some residents have lost the joy of life as a result.

Depending on the situation, medication could support their psychological well-being.

Visits from relatives, friends or a professional also help the residents. After a visit, the residents are often more balanced and satisfied.

1.8. Grief counselling

There are various circumstances that cause difficulties for people entering a care institution:

- Being in a new place
- Dependency
- Loss of self-determination
- Giving up / loss of their "home"
- Loss of cognitive skills
- Death of a partner
- Health restrictions
- Loneliness

All these circumstances can make it more difficult for the residents to find the purpose and drive needed to continue living happily and they can make it difficult to participate in care home life. They withdraw into themselves. It takes a lot of understanding, patience, and time on the part of the staff, relatives and professionals. The residents need a lot of attention and people to listen to them so that they can get their worries off their minds. Sometimes talking, listening to music together or alone, taking a walk in nature or, as mentioned above, medication can help.

When my father-in-law was in a nursing home, I wrote his biography with him. It was a rewarding way to distract him.

1.9. Personal responsibility

If residents are still physically and cognitively able to take part in various activities, such as going outside with a stick or walking frame they may still need encouragement to be motivated to do so.

I have noticed that those residents, who take some responsibility for their day to day lives, are more satisfied and have a higher quality of life because they have some control and can help shape the structure of their days. When people are in constant pain however, it takes a very strong will, not to give up. The residents then often say: "What for?"

Often one succeeds in motivating the residents and luring them out of their mental prison by encouraging them to take a walk or have a coffee so that they have a change of scenery.
If this doesn't work or is not possible, sitting with them and chatting can be a potential distraction. Above all, proper listening is required, because what the residents lack is a meaningful conversation where someone really gives them their full time and attention. Many have told me that they miss interaction with like-minded people.

Often all they have left is the television! Whether this can meet their needs or just helps them bridge the hours until dinner?

If residents consciously refuse all offers of activities and interactions given by the home or another professional, this must be respected. One can gently make them aware of the possible consequences of their actions, but in the end the decision is theirs.

However, it is also important that the residents take on a certain amount of personal responsibility for their actions or for inaction.

I gently point out to residents every now and then that if they do not stay active, their mobility and therefore their quality-of-life, could be massively restricted.

1.10. Acceptance and reorientation

A wonderful example of the benefits of acceptance and reorientation was a resident I met, who had been confined to a wheelchair due to illness.

She entered the nursing home with her husband. Both participated in various home activities. However, at some point her husband's condition worsened and he died.

Despite her sad situation, the resident kept her positive disposition. Her hobby, sewing, kept her busy. She used to sew clothes and traditional costumes for dolls.

Since she was a gifted seamstress, she was asked if she would like to alter or mend the clothes of other residents, which she accepted with thanks. She also helped to create various table decorations.

She didn't let her situation get her down. She took part in events, liked to play cards and if you asked her how she was, you always got a positive answer.
The resident had come to terms with her condition and in my opinion, she was a role model for many of how she had accepted her situation and found a new meaning in life. She made her life meaningful and her hobbies were her anchor, where she found peace.

Why is it, that some people, despite unlucky circumstances, manage to remain positive and some not? My impression is that people who have a strong social network adapt better to a new situation. They often receive visitors, can exchange ideas and discuss their worries and joys with their loved ones.

Over these many years I have mostly accompanied people who have had no relatives, whose friends live further away or are no longer mobile. In any case, they are residents who have received few or no visitors at all.

They were all so happy and grateful for a visit.
In my experience, it seems that people who have had to struggle early in their life, be it for health or family reasons, can adapt better to emerging challenges even after challenging situations, such as entering a home. If their health still allows, they take advantage of the resources available.

During my visits I have noticed that people who for whatever reason cannot or do not want to join in with the activities, even if they still can do so, often react with depressive moods and struggle with them again and again.

It is never easy to motivate them to do something that brings them joy and distraction or that changes the way they see things. They are stuck and sometimes the only thing that can help is medication to lift their mood a little.

Part 2
Illness and fears

Every person is unique, and a disease progresses differently in each person for a variety of reasons. Therefore, everyday life in the nursing home is also different for everyone.
There are some residents who have been in a nursing home for many years and hardly need any help. However, depending on the progression of their illness or their age they may of course become increasingly and at some point, permanently dependent on the help of the staff and walking frames may become their constant companion. Phases of feeling settled can alternate with more unsettled phases. It may well be that a resident feels better about being in the care home sometimes and worse at others.

Often a person loses their independence bit by bit. As a result, many residents feel that they are becoming an unnecessary burden for relatives and the care team, be it financially, organisationally or emotionally. The increasing dependence is a great psychological burden for some residents.

Dignified, attentive, supportive, and strengthening interaction with the relatives, the nursing staff or an accompanying professional is essential.
In these moments, it is important to promote and discuss advantages and not just see any negatives.

There is a direct link between mental health and self-esteem.

If the sick person does not have a well-functioning, supportive, social network, this can aggravate or accelerate their decline. The resident becomes lethargic and withdraws into themselves until they fall completely silent. I find it very upsetting that some residents do not receive any or very few visitors!

Over the years I built up a valuable relationship with some of the residents and I was allowed to accompany some of them in their dying process until they had left this world.

I would like to give you an example here, from an elderly man who almost never had visitors. I first saw him as I walked down the corridor at the care home. I saw him sitting on a couch, leaning on his walking stick and greeted him. He never spoke or said hello back.

One day I felt the impulse to sit next to him. I asked him if this was ok and since he showed no reaction, I sat quietly next to him for a while. Then I said goodbye again. He mumbled something into his beard and I left. This was repeated on a next visit. The third time I started a conversation with him. He had worked on various farms so we talked about farm life. Over time he opened up. From then on he said goodbye, waved to me with a smile on his face and asked when I would be back.

I was allowed to accompany this man in his dying phase up to his death. I will never forget the way he caressed my arms with his hands towards the end of his life and thanked me for everything. That touched me very much.

It shows once again how valuable it is when people still have a well-functioning social network.

2.1. Fears of loss, despair

There are different types of losses:
Loss of a job, of loved ones, of pets, of skills, of a home, of health as well as of independence.

A younger person is more likely to be able to cope with such losses. Often an older person no longer has the psychological strength to compensate for this and begins to brood or despair, as they suffer from these losses.

These are difficult experiences in the last phase of life! Many residents struggle with this. Their desperation shows up in different ways. Some people are more withdrawn, thoughtful, quiet and at a loss, while others are more frustrated and angry.

Residents who suffer from long term illnesses may have to learn to accept their state of illness as permanent. Relatives, caregivers or a professional may be able to distract them for a few hours, but they must go through the inner process of acceptance on their own.

I cannot say enough that stable, warm, supportive relationships are key resources for maintaining mental health.

2.2. Forgetfulness and dementia

Forgetfulness

Age-related forgetfulness is not due to illness, but rather a slight cognitive impairment. It has a slow course and is not to be equated with dementia.

Dementia

Dementia is an umbrella term that encompasses more than 50 different, chronically progressive diseases of the cerebrum. These lead to damage to the brain tissue and the loss of nerve cells.

Here is a brief description of two types of dementia: Alzheimer's dementia and vascular dementia

Alzheimer's dementia

* *Alzheimer's dementia is a degenerative form of dementia. More than half of all people with dementia are affected by this form.*

It creeps up on those affected. The first symptoms are usually memory problems or word finding problems. There are changes in mood and behavior, with sufferers becoming listless, depressed and withdrawn. In the course of the disease, more and more nerve cells die in certain sections of the cerebrum. The brain volume can shrink by up to 20%. Alzheimer's dementia remains incurable.
Coping with everyday life becomes harder. Those affected are increasingly dependent on support. At the

onset of dementia, those affected consciously experience that they are forgetting something. This feeling of memory loss can trigger different emotions such as fear, despair, anger, etc. Despite the losses, Alzheimer sufferers may still have a great deal of independence and competences that need to be recognized and put to use.

* *Source: Alzheimer Switzerland, information sheet Frequent Dementia Diseases, www.alz.ch*

Vascular dementia

* *In contrast to Alzheimer's dementia, vascular dementia is not a degenerative dementia. Recurring small strokes or cerebral hemorrhages cause damage in various brain regions. However, the cognitive abilities do not decrease between these "slumps". Often those affected only feel a deterioration after a further stroke. These can be minor or very drastic. Life is thus mixed-up bit by bit.*

Vascular dementia is therefore more of a staircase. The symptoms vary widely and it is difficult to describe this form of dementia in stages. The people concerned often need clear routines and a daily structure that they are familiar with.

* *Source: Alzheimer Switzerland, information sheet Frequent Dementia Diseases, www.alz.ch*

In all these years I have learned something important from talking to people with dementia. You can't rush a conversation when someone has dementia.

People with dementia take a long time to communicate with a person. They need time to think about what they would like to express. I've got into the habit of allowing enough time for them so that an encounter takes place that is fulfilling for both parties and not tedious and tiring.

Dealing with people with dementia requires tact and awareness. Dementia sufferers are often very intuitively aware when others are finding it difficult to understand them. Other people's moods and reactions can have a strong effect on them.
When I'm nervous during such a conversation, there is no real connection possible. I have found when I am calm it is much easier to communicate.
Depending on the stage of dementia, people with dementia repeat themselves again and again in stories (often going back to childhood).
It takes a lot of patience and genuine interest because dementia sufferers sense whether it is a heart-to-heart communication or not.

Dementia is a great challenge for everyone involved. People with dementia are often stuck in their own world (often going back to childhood), far removed from reality. Dealing with dementia is incredibly difficult requiring a lot of commitment and leaves one feeling sad, frustrated and hopeless.
Relatives lose a loved one in installments!

However, it is important to remember, that it is only the mind that suffers with dementia and not the heart. What I mean by this is, even if some people with dementia can no longer communicate verbally, they intuitively perceive how we deal with them. We cannot pretend. They notice every change in mood, no matter how small.

2.3. Coping with difficult situations

There are so many difficult situations that residents and relatives have to cope with, for example:

- A permanent move into a care home
- A partner's death
- Acute progression of an illness
- Resident's illness becomes terminal
- Gradual loss of memory
- Loneliness

There are many ways to reflect, tackle and resolve a difficult situation.

In all these years in which I have accompanied people, I have noticed that residents and relatives have used different strategies to cope with their difficulties.

Some suppress reality because they cannot endure the situation in which they find themselves or cannot face the truth. It is a temporary survival strategy, because otherwise the pain would be overwhelming.

Not only residents, but also relatives may struggle with the constantly changing situations. Sometimes events happen in rapid succession, so that those involved do not have time to adjust.

2.4. Dependence and loss of dignity

Dependency and loss of dignity are delicate points that should be handled sensitively.

When a person enters a care institution, it is possible that due to an illness or an accident they can no longer feed themselves, shower alone or must be accompanied to the toilet.

The resident becomes dependent and must ask the staff for help, which initially embarrasses them and causes them difficulties.

It takes a lot of sensitivity and understanding on the part of the staff.

If a person needs help with eating, for example because of a stroke, the staff need a lot of patience, time and understanding.

When residents first need help, feelings of powerlessness, shame and inner conflicts can arise. In this phase, it is particularly important to be careful and respectful of their dignity.
It is helpful when relatives do not downplay these circumstances, but rather signal that they understand their loved ones and how they are feeling.

2.5. Visits, how often?

One topic that needs to be looked at is around visiting a resident of a care home.

The deterioration of the resident's condition can also psychologically affect relatives. It is important that the relative consciously designs their own life so that they do not forget themselves. It is not selfish if relatives take care of themselves in between visits, so that they can maintain their emotional balance.

Many life partners visit their loved ones every day and have a guilty conscience if they do not come. I believe that the relatives should deliberately not visit at least one or two days a week, even if this meets with resistance from their loved ones.

They must not forget themselves and should continue to maintain their social contacts.

The visiting relative could gently discuss with their love one why and when they need their day off. The relatives can, for example, choose days on which the care home offers activities, so the absence of a partner is not so important for the residents.

It is a good idea for the relative to always choose the same days when they stay away. This generates a regularity that is helpful not only for the residents, but also for the staff.

Part 3
Dying process / Dying phases / Symptoms

Very few people die the way they wish, namely that they simply don't wake up one morning!

Everyone dies differently and at a different pace.

In the dying phase, people's behavior changes, which can indicate approaching death.
It is helpful for loved ones to know that a person can seem to blossom a few days before death. They eat again and seem to be feeling a bit better. Unfortunately, this improved period is very short.

I have often observed that people in the dying phase keep their eyes closed for increasingly long periods even though they are awake. They are just weak.

Nevertheless, they are happy when the relatives speak to them and tell them something or sing.

With every dying person I had the feeling that people intuitively sensed early on in this "dying phase" that they will die soon, even if some of them refused to admit it until the end.

I also believe that people who have been introverts in life are more likely to die in their sleep than people who have always fought in life.
These people often fight in the dying phase.

Relatives should be prepared for the fact that this time can be a tiring and challenging journey for everyone involved. Some relatives told me in retrospect that it was very exhausting for them. Nevertheless, this time was necessary and valuable for them so that they could slowly say goodbye to their loved ones.

Some people can leave the physical world calmly. They have settled all written matters, funeral requests, resolved any disputes and said goodbye to their loved ones.

However, there are also people who fight for days or weeks until they die. They do not want to or cannot die for a variety of reasons because they may be plagued by fears such as:

- They haven't settled everything
- They are still waiting for someone to say goodbye to them
- They still want to forgive someone or they want someone to forgive them
- They are simply afraid of dying

Even if loved ones struggle to forgive a dying mother or father because the issues are too great. I would still advise giving it a try.
Forgiveness brings peace!

Maybe it would be healing for both parties if the relative could tell the dying person their feelings and to tell them everything is now fine and they can now go or let go.

Often the dying people have the feeling that they are not allowed to go because of the relatives' presence and only let go when the relatives leave the room.

The relatives need not have a guilty conscience that they left the room, because it is likely that the dying person has made a conscious decision to die alone when no one is in the room!

3.1. The 5 Stages of Dying

(Elisabeth Kübler-Ross model, Swiss-American psychiatrist)

Phase 1: Denial

Almost all patients try to deny the terminal diagnosis to themselves, not only when first diagnosed, but again and again later.

Phase 2: Anger

Why me? Why not XYZ? The anger is often directed towards the staff: the nursing staff and the doctor are no good!

Phase 3: Bargaining

The third phase, which is usually only a fleeting one, is less well known, but is often very helpful for the patient. If in the first phase we are unable to acknowledge the facts and in the second, we quarrel with God and the world, in the third we may try to postpone the inevitable through a kind of "deal with God". Basically, a patient bargains for a delay.

Phase 4: Depression

If the terminally ill can no longer deny their illness, if new interventions and hospital stays are necessary, if they become weaker and more miserable, then they cannot always dismiss their condition with a smile. Intense rage and anger soon give way to a feeling of terrible loss.

Phase 5: Acceptance

If the patient has enough time and does not suddenly die, if they have found help to overcome Phase 1, they reach a stage in which they no longer accept their fate dejectedly or angrily. They were allowed to express their emotions, their envy of the living and healthy, the anger of all who do not see their death so close in front of them. They have mourned the impending loss of so many loved ones and places, and now they are looking forward to the end with calm expectation. They are tired, usually very weak and have the need to doze off or sleep often with only short intervals awake.

It is a different sleep than in the time of the depression, it is no longer used for breathing in between attacks of pain, it is no longer evasive and no longer a break for relaxation; but now the need gradually grows to lengthen the hours of sleep as in the case of a newborn, only with the opposite meaning. This phase is free from feelings. Now comes the time of final rest before the long journey. In this phase, the relatives often need more support and understanding than the patient themselves.

Source: The books: On Death and Dying / Death The Final Stage of Growth

During my care of those who are terminally ill, I have experienced that, firstly, these 5 phases are not always lived through and, secondly, not they do not always happen in the order of 1-5, but can be mixed up and / or recurring.

There are also these 5 phases with the mourners.

When adult children find out, for example, that one of their parents has cancer and will die very soon, or when a relative experiences that their partner has had a severe stroke, Elisabeth Kübler-Ross speaks of pre-grief, which is an important part of the experience of the loss. It is part of the process for those faced with death of a loved one. It is the beginning of the grieving process. Such pre-mourning can help prepare one for what is to come.
But one should be prepared that anticipating an event can be as overwhelming as the event itself.

Being forewarned doesn't always mean being prepared. This experience may or may not ease or shorten the process of grieving.
But it can also make one feel guilty because one grieves before the loss has occurred. One can experience all 5 phases of grief before death occurs. Here, too, it can be

that one will only experience the phases of anger and denial (not wanting it to be true).
In some cases, grief can start years before the loss, such as Alzheimer's or MS multiple sclerosis, where loved ones are lost little by little.

3.2. Possible symptoms during the dying process

For the elderly dying can often be a lengthy process. The dying patient may experience some or more of the following symptoms:

- General weakness in speaking, in fixing eyes or in swallowing
- Physical restlessness, tugging on bedding / nightdress, trying to get out of bed
- More sleep phases than awake phases
- Periods of unconsciousness, varying in depth
- Cold extremities, marbled skin due to poor circulation (towards the end)
- Death triangle: white discoloration around the nose and mouth
- Urinary retention, incontinence
- Change in breathing ⋆, irregular breathing, rattle breathing ⋆, gasping breath ⋆
- Respiratory and cardiac arrest (clinical death)
- Rigid pupils, failure of the central nervous system (biological death)
- Last radio signal from the brain stem: After the last breath, another "supposedly last breath" can follow a few minutes later. It is important to know so that relatives can prepare for it and not be frightened.

**Change in breathing: In the last hours of life, breathing also changes. Breathing pauses of up to 50 seconds can occur, then breathing starts again.*

**Rattle breathing: The rattle occurs because the dying person can no longer swallow or cough, which is why the mucus oscillates back and forth with the breath. There is no shortness of breath, and it is not painful. However, relatives are often frightened because they have never heard such rattling breaths and believe that the dying person suffocates, which is not the case.*

At this point in time, the dying person should not be given any more fluids, only the mouth should be moistened with a spray.

**Gasping: Shortly before the final cessation of breathing, gasping can often be observed It is characterized by individual snapping breaths with long pauses between them.*

3.3. Physical and mental support

There are different ways to support a person physically and mentally in the dying phase:

- Avoid their exertion
- Create a pleasant, calm atmosphere, no restlessness or hectic behaviour
- Frequent mouth, lip, and eye care
- Refreshments in the form of washes and rubs with usual lotions
- Changes of position to keep them comfortable
- Frequent changes of clothes when sweating, warm blanket when shivering

- Offer their favorite drink, if still possible, or use it to moisten the lip and mouth
- If breathing is difficult, give oxygen, remove mucus from mouth, keep upper body a little raised
- The sense of hearing is the last sense that disappears, so always speak in the presence of the dying person as if they were fully conscious. Please do not talk about activities such as funeral formalities after the death, in front of the dying person!
  (A relative once asked me in the dying room whether the dying person still needed his watch on his wrist!)
- The dying understand, even if they can no longer react
- The dying should be spoken to with understanding
- The dying send out signals, for example, when someone withdraws their hand, understand and accept this
- The dying are withdrawing more and more from their environment
- If possible, address the needs or wishes of the dying person and let them choose who should visit rather than it be the relative's choice
- Allow privacy, perhaps only with close relatives, friends or a professional in the last stages

Part 4
Fear / End-of-life care / Grief counselling

4.1. Fear of dying

For many people dying and death are threatening and frightening.

If I had not been able to get to know someone, before I was allowed to accompany them on their last journey, I sometimes asked myself how the dying person would judge their situation? Do they deny it, do they accept it and will they surrender to it? What thoughts and feelings accompany the dying person in his process? What are their fears? Are they consciously experiencing the process? Were they able or willing to talk about their fears beforehand?

It would be so beneficial if everybody could talk about their fears. However, depending on the personality of those involved, this is not always possible.

Many people are afraid if they are left alone in the dying phase. A companion can take away some of the fear. Whenever possible, end-of-life support should be offered so that the person concerned does not have to die alone.

During the dying process, I have only been able to speak to a few dying people about their fears.
The idea of suffering excruciating pain often scares the dying, more than dying itself.

If a person is allowed or able to express their fear of dying, the relatives or a professional can support them and, above all, if the person dying can understand their feelings, this helps them during the dying process and they become calmer.

The fears of the dying have many facets:

- Fear of how relatives will manage after their death
- Fear of pain
- Fear of the unresolved
- Fear of being alone
- Fear of separation
- Fear of the unknown

I remember one incident:
I visited a woman for the first time, introduced myself and we started a conversation. I soon realized that she had a burning question on her mind:
"Can't I stop eating?"
I then asked her if she no longer wanted to eat, to which she said no. Then I asked her directly if she would like to die, which she answered in the affirmative! She didn't dare to just stop eating and still needed confirmation that it would be okay if she stopped eating. Her mind was clear and she told me that she had arranged everything with her children. Then she closed her eyes and became very calm.
I said goodbye to her soon afterwards and wished her a good journey, even though I hadn't thought at the time that she would 'leave' us so quickly. She opened her eyes and smiled. She died two days after my visit.

The relatives often swing between hope and fear. It is very important to keep the relatives calm so that their fear does not spread to the dying person.

My last dying companion in the nursing home was a resident, whose dying process was, in my opinion, a perfect textbook example. The resident was able to discuss her fears with her daughter and was in the fortunate position of going through the dying process very consciously and without strong pain medication. Until a few hours before she died, she could nod when I asked her a question or explained what tasks I was going to do.

But there are also relatives who cannot respect the father's or mother's wish to die and instead suppress reality and do not want to admit it. They want more medical treatment for the resident and are not ready to accept the reality. It's a difficult situation for everyone involved. But with professional care, good conversations often result and relatives then think about the need to let their loved ones go.

The first time I accompanied a person with severe pain on his last journey, I panicked.
It was my first professional end-of-life care for a person in great pain. The dying man was in so much pain that he grabbed my sweater and cried out for help. I felt overwhelmed by the situation. After the nurses gave him pain medication, the dying man slowly calmed down.

How difficult must such a situation be for relatives?

My view is that when a person is not in pain, they go through the process of dying consciously. The dying person is sometimes only sedated because the relatives cannot endure this process and the 'restlessness'.

Even if a dying person can no longer express their wishes verbally, for example can no longer speak, they can still show that they do not want to be touched. They flinch or move their body or their hand or pull away if they still have the strength! Therefore, the companion should be very careful with their own impulse to touch and not enforce their own personal wishes.

Through the many dying processes I accompanied, I became aware of how challenging terminal care can be for relatives. During this process, the relatives not only have to deal with their feelings and fear of loss, but also experience how painful a dying process can be for their loved ones.

Relatives of the dying also often experience a rollercoaster of emotions because they feel abandoned and alone.

As already mentioned, the relatives can also go through the 5 phases of mourning (see Section 3.1 above).

4.2. End-of-life care

Either before or at the start of the dying phase, the nursing staff, the specialist for terminal care or a pastor can provide the residents the opportunity to tell them what their wishes are for their dying phase, their beliefs, their convictions and values, everything that is important to them.

It is essential to see a dying patient in their uniqueness and to respect them as an individual. Then the best companion can be chosen to be present for the dying phase and the dying person's wishes best fulfilled.

If possible, the dying should be left in their usual environment and not moved to another room.

In my opinion, the most important thing about end-of-life care is that all activities are carried out calmly. There should be no hectic activity or unrest because this can be unsettling to the dying.
An atmosphere should be created that makes it easier for the dying to die.

The relatives often set up the room in such a way that a loving, warm, peaceful atmosphere is created.

When relatives cannot let go of the dying loved one, it is very difficult for the person to surrender to the natural process of dying.
It takes courage and strength to be able to tell a dying person that they are loved and to let them go in love so that they can die quietly and pass into a dimension that is still unknown to the living.
Terminal care should always be carried out in the interests of the dying person. Their wishes should be respected, including wishes of a religious nature, such as the anointing of the sick or the wish for a clergyperson.
If the companion knows the person's preferences and knows what music they like, then they can play the corresponding music or sing to them.

It is very helpful to know the preferences of a dying person and know in advance that they for example, like to drink coke. One could moisten their mouth with coke. If they can no longer drink, wrap a small ice cube made of cola in gauze and rub the mouth with it.
When I am providing care for the dying, I ask for support in meditation, especially if I do not know someone. My personal spiritual support, attitude and behaviour create a peaceful, calm atmosphere. Every now and then I ask a dying person whether I can touch their arm or hand. In this way I can calm them down.

If a dying person can no longer express their wishes verbally, they can still show that they do not want to be touched. They move their body or their hand – sometimes barely visibly.
It is very important that a companion always tells the dying person their intentions, such as giving them something to drink, moistening their mouth, putting cream on their lips, putting a damp cloth on their forehead, etc., because they still understand what is being said.

If the dying person closes their mouth tightly and does not want anything more to drink, this should be respected, because they may no longer be able to swallow. If something is poured into them, they could suffocate, because at this point, they no longer have the strength to cough it up. All a companion should do is moisten their mouth with a spray bottle or wet sponges on sticks and apply cream to their lips so that the mouth area remains moist, the tongue does not dry out and the lips remain supple so that there are no cracks.

Many relatives are happy when they can do something, even if it is just a small amount of care, such as moistening their mouths or dabbing their foreheads with a cloth. Doing nothing is often difficult to bear and the relatives feel helpless.

They are also grateful when they can talk to a professional about their fears and concerns.

When the dying hear the voices of loved ones, it sometimes calms them down. This gives them the reassurance that they are not alone.
In the advanced process of dying, a person can smell strongly of acetone. I suggest the companion try holding a tissue sprayed with lavender oil to their own nose as discretely as possible, to make it easier for them to breathe.

4.3. Grief counselling for relatives

During a dying process, it is important that the relatives are also well looked after, as they too are in a vulnerable situation.

Every situation is different. There are relatives who are grateful and relieved when a professional accompanies their loved one on their last journey alongside the relative. The relative may feel more secure and less afraid of the unknown. They can then ask questions and not feel left alone in their pain. Accompanying them enables them to say goodbye in a calm manner.

Relatives often find it difficult to have a professional accompany for their loved ones during the night. The relatives are torn between the fear and their guilty conscience that their loved ones could die in the night without them being there. Understandably, it is difficult for them to admit to themselves that they cannot sit by the bed of their loved ones day and night.

I talk to relatives again and again and softly point out, that the dying phase could possibly last a few days and that it is important to rest at night to keep up their strength.

The relatives are grateful if they can talk to a professional about their fears.

It is important that relatives are cared for even after a loved one has passed away.

The ways of mourning and saying goodbye are very individual. Often the relatives feel lost after the death of their loved ones and so overwhelmed by their grief that they can no longer think clearly.

They may be grateful if they are not left alone but are given quiet time to collect themselves. They may need someone to listen to them or to discuss what is on their minds in this highly emotional situation.

Part 5
Culture of mourning / Tools for relatives to deal with grief

5.1. Culture of mourning

The culture of mourning is currently in a state of upheaval. Old traditions are being abandoned. At a funeral, black is often no longer worn, and the black button on the suit (as a sign of mourning) and the mourning ribbon have also disappeared. New expressions of grief are emerging such as a celebration of a person's life. As a rule, they are more individualistic than the sometimes rather rigid patterns and rituals of the past.

Unfortunately, this has the consequence that in many countries in today's secular times, mourning has become more private and suppressed as death is a topic that is publicly avoided. Who wants to be confronted with the subject of death and their own inevitable mortality?

Therefore, people mourning these days tend to keep themselves busy, although they would much rather withdraw. They often avoid talking about the deceased and go about their daily duties, although their thoughts may wander again and again to their grief.
Even when society and individuals do not allow the necessary time to grieve, the relative continues to feel the loss, the pain, and the fear. A bereaved body reacts accordingly. One cannot sleep, has no appetite and cannot concentrate.

Since mourners are often given far too few opportunities to speak about their loss and show their grief, they avoid dealing with death.
I have observed that a grieving process has to be actively lived through to be able to come to terms with a loss. You can't just wait for time to heal the grief and wounds because it doesn't. The grieving should not be postponed until later, otherwise the healing process will also be postponed until later.

Condolence visits can really help a mourner to grieve. It sometimes helps when a bereaved is not left alone at this difficult emotional time.

I remember when someone from my circle of acquaintances suffered a loss, he mentioned that he not only missed the deceased, but also felt quite abandoned by his circle of friends after the funeral. He would have liked to have received more visits from others beside his close relatives. He found it difficult to bear the many hours that he spent alone. He almost couldn't bear the emptiness and the pain that he couldn't share.

Ignoring death also means avoiding condolence visits. People no longer know how to approach someone who is grieving! But hardly anyone is aware of how painful and incomprehensible it is for those grieving when people stay away.
It is very important to know that people who have lost a loved one are unlikely to come to you. They will neither make phone calls nor come over for a visit.

Even if the mourners do not make contact themselves, they may be extremely grateful when they receive a visit and can talk about the deceased.

It is a kindness to take the first step, call, visit, ask sensitive questions and find out what they need.

In certain cultures, the mourners are not left alone in the first few weeks but are cooked for and looked after by the family and friends.

A grieving person is so caught up in grief for the first few weeks or even months that he or she does not have the strength to turn to others.

5.2. Tools for relatives to deal with grief

Some rituals that give comfort and support:

- Choose a photo of the deceased person and talk to them about how you are feeling
- Write a letter to a loved one who has died and write everything that is in your mind that brings relief, be it sadness, anger or joy, helplessness, fear, loneliness, despair, powerlessness. Write to them about what could not be said or done in their lifetime. Expressing gratitude, addressing hurts, breaking the silence, etc.
- Go to the grave, light a candle and get in touch with the deceased.
- Go into nature, talk to the deceased and evoke memories of shared, beautiful experiences.

- Thank them for the wonderful time you had the privilege to spend with them.
- According to the grieving persons faith or beliefs it could be comforting for them to consider that the deceased now lives in the spiritual world, that they are doing well there and that they can communicate with them.
- Talk to the deceased before going to sleep.
- Asking the deceased to be with you always in love.

Epilogue

Medical science has made great strides, so that we humans are living longer and dying much older. This is not the fault of the elderly, but the consequence of progress.

Technology is a blessing because it saves lives.
In my opinion, in old age it is important that the quality of life is improved through treatment or surgery and not just that life is prolonged. If possible, everybody should think seriously in advance about which health treatment or procedures they would be prepared to undergo.

What the many older people have taught me over the years are:

Patience – letting go – acceptance.

This is the fine art of old age!

Acknowledgements

I want you to know how invaluable each and every support has been to me, be it your encouragement to publish this guide, the expertise, editing, proofreading, the personal stories that I was allowed to publish and the great, spontaneous help translating from German to English. A big thank you from the bottom of my heart!

The author

Brigitta Rhyner was born and raised in Zurich in 1956. She has lived in Felben-Wellhausen for over thirty years. She is married and has two sons.
She discovered her love for languages and different cultures during her annual language stays in a Francophone territory and in England. She lived with her husband in Sweden, Jemen, and America. Her interest and love for different cultures, people and travel has remained to this day.
In 2011 Brigitta completed a three-year training as a death and grief counsellor and has since accompanied people in the last phase of their life.
The joys and sorrows in a nursing home, dying and death have been an integral part of her life for ten years.
Following the training, Brigitta has completed various advanced training courses, in which she has acquired in-depth knowledge of the topics of energy treatments, kinesiological trauma decoupling, spiritual healing and trance healing. She has been practicing in Felben since 2014.